DOROTHY IS MOVING MOUNTAINS

WRITTEN BY DOROTHY PAAD
ILLUSTRATED BY MATTHEW FORGRAVE
EDITED BY BRANDY THOMAS
LAYOUT BY TRAVIS GERHART, LAKE SUPERIOR PRESS, MARQUETTE, MI
ISBN: 978-1-7375014-2-8
LIBRARY OF CONGRESS CONTROL NUMBER: 2022921911

ALL RIGHTS RESERVED. NO PART OF THIS PUBLICATION MAY BE REPRODUCED, DISTRIBUTED, OR TRANSMITTED IN ANY FORM, OR BY ANY MEANS, OR STORED IN A DATABASE OR RETRIEVAL SYSTEM WITHOUT THE PRIOR WRITTEN PERMISSION OF THE PUBLISHER.

COPYRIGHT © 2022 DOROTHY PAAD

PUBLISHED BY DEP BOOKS, LLC
PO BOX 637, MARQUETTE, MI 49855

PRINTED IN THE UNITED STATES OF AMERICA

TO PURCHASE ADDITIONAL BOOKS,
PLEASE VISIT OUR WEBSITE AT DEPBOOKS.COM

About the Author

Dorothy Paad loves to create — whether it is a song, a dance, a theater production, or book. She doesn't let having Cerebral Palsy stand in her way! It was during the COVID-19 pandemic that Dorothy was inspired to write her first book hoping to inspire kids in a way she wishes she had been. Today, she continues to share her story so that others may realize their potential and never stop pursuing their dreams.

Dorothy puts her heart and soul into all that she does. Each of her books reflects important moments in her life and highlights the people who have supported her along the way. Among the many people that have inspired her work are her father, Eric and brother, Andrew, who served in the United States Air Force and United States Army respectively; and her best friend and role model, Alice, whom she calls, Mom.

In addition to her work in the writing and performing arts, Dorothy also works as an advocate for individuals with disabilities and caregivers as the spokesperson for the Caregiver Incentive Project. Her own in-home caregiver, Tracy, makes a valuable difference in her life — helping her to live her life to the fullest. In an effort to prepare future teachers for inclusive classrooms, Dorothy is also an Instructional Coach for the Northern Michigan University School of Education.

She is the recipient of a MI-UCP (United Cerebral Palsy Association) Closing the Disability Divide Award and a volunteer with Lake Superior Life Care & Hospice. Dorothy is also a member of the Upper Peninsula Publishers & Authors Association and Marquette Alger Reading Council.

Dorothy loves to read, learn about history, and participate in the performing arts. She also enjoys traveling — counting among her favorite trips, London, and visits to various Disney theme parks. In her free time, Dorothy also finds enjoyment in exploring the Internet and watching her favorite TV shows and movies. Having been born and raised in Washington State, Dorothy now lives in the Upper Peninsula of Michigan in the city of Marquette.

moving mountains
adaptive program
movingmountainsap.org

To Bud and Denise Delano-
angels on earth, who helped me find my courage,
and moved mountains for me.

Dorothy and her dad were at
the Physical Therapist or PT for short.

The PT was a special doctor who helped Dorothy learn
to move her legs and helped them not be sore.
Cerebral palsy sometimes makes your muscles sore.

To help you, the exercises the PT makes you do sometimes hurt.
To distract Dorothy, Dad was chatting with the PT.
Dad is very good at chatting. So is Dorothy.

The PT asked, "Dorothy, what do you like to do outside the house for fun?"

Dorothy replied, "Nothing. I feel lonely, but I don't think I can do anything."

Dorothy remembered all the bullies, the people in high school who said she couldn't do anything because she was disabled.

Mom and Dad tried to help.
They knew that those people were wrong in what they said.

But Dorothy was still sad.
She had no confidence.
She didn't feel she could do anything.

The PT said, "That's a shame, Dorothy. I have some friends who teach adaptive skiing. You should try it!"

Dorothy asked, "What is adaptive skiing?"

The PT replied, "It's kinda like sledding down a mountain- only most people stand up when they ski. You'd sit down."

Dorothy exclaimed, "Oh, that sounds fun! I want to try."

Dad looked puzzled.
Sometimes, because of something called a sensory disorder,
Dorothy was afraid of things like fast movement, or loud noises.

Besides, Dorothy liked the fine arts, music, dance, and theater more than she liked sports and playing outside.

"Are you sure?" asked Dad.

Dorothy was determined, "Yes!" she said.
So, the PT gave Dad the phone number.

Later, at home, Dad called the number.

A nice polar bear named Denise picked up the phone.
Mom, Dad, and Dorothy lived in the forest near the mountains.
Denise and her husband Bud lived in the
cold snowy forest at the base of the mountains.

Denise had all kinds of questions.
Mom, Dad, and Dorothy did too.

Denise sent all kinds of paperwork; questions about Dorothy, safety, and emergency forms, contact information for Mom and Dad, etc.
Mom helped Dorothy fill them out.

Then Denise called with a date to go skiing,

Mom took Dorothy shopping.
They had to get a coat, hat, gloves, and snow pants.

Finally, the big day came.
Off to the snowy mountains they went.
Dorothy had mixed emotions.
She wanted to have fun, but she feared how fast she would go,
or falling over and getting hurt.
Plus, she didn't know the ski instructors. She had separation anxiety.
That means that even though Dorothy was a grown-up moose,
she got nervous meeting new adults,
and being away from Mom and Dad.
But they wouldn't be too far away.

The ski lodge had tons of activity.
It looked like a winter wonderland.

Bud and Denise came over to say hi.
They were very friendly polar bears.
Just being around them made Dorothy feel happier and safe.

Bud was going to be one of Dorothy's ski instructors.
She had two for safety, one to teach and give directions,
and one to watch, to make sure no one got hurt.
Denise was going to stay at the bottom of
the ski hill with Mom and Dad and watch.

Mom and Dad helped Dorothy get dressed in her winter clothes.
Bud put a helmet on Dorothy to protect her head in case she fell.

Then Bud and Dad helped her into the sit-ski
which reminded her of Santa's sleigh on skis.
There were lots of straps for her chest, legs, and arms.
Dorothy liked the feeling. It helped her not worry about falling.
She also knew Bud was going to be tethered to her;
he was going to be connected to the sit-ski by a rope.
That made her feel better.

They met Nick, a photographer.
He was going to take pictures and video of Dorothy skiing.
He was also a very nice polar bear. Dorothy was impressed.
He knew how to ski backwards while holding a big camera,
without falling or running into trees.

The first part of going skiing was the ski lift.
Dorothy's sit-ski would be attached to the ski lift chair
and lifted up the mountain the same as all the other skiers.
Dorothy wasn't sure about the height but as long as she was
talking to the ski instructors and didn't look down, she was OK.

They got to the tippity top of the mountain.
BUMP went Dorothy as she transferred off the ski lift to the ground.

There were three types of trails down the mountain.
Green for easy; blue, medium; and black diamond, hard.
Dorothy wanted to try easy first.

Bud had some directions for Dorothy:
when he said left it meant point and lean to the left;
center meant sit up straight;
and right meant point and lean to the right.
They practiced before going down the trail.
They also practiced how to fall.
Dorothy knew Bud was right there to keep her safe.

Down they went.
It was fast, but Dorothy wasn't scared. It was fun.
Was she perfect? No.
But that was OK.
Did she fall? Yes.
But she wasn't hurt.
So, she got up and kept going.

"Woo-hoo!" Dorothy yelled.
She met Mom and Dad at the bottom.
She told them that if she can do this, she could do anything.

Back up she went.
When she was ready, after a few lessons,
she got to try the black diamond.
That was so much fun and fast!

And that's how Dorothy found her confidence.
Always be the best you and believe in yourself,
that you can do anything!!!

Although the first time the term sit-ski was used in print was in the Ludington, MI Daily News, it was patented by an Austrian ski manufacturer, Engelbert Brenter on March 10, 1949. It was described by the Ludington Daily News as "a ski with a seat fitted on top; specifically; one designed to be used by skiers with limited or no mobility in their legs."